William Bolcom

T0088340

Primer and Other Duets for One Piano/Four Hands

ISBN 978-1-5400-0036-1

EDWARD B. MARKS MUSIC COMPANY / EXCLUSIVELY DISTRIBUTED BY HAL•LEONARD®

www.ebmarks.com
www.halleonard.com

CONTENTS

PRIMER

1   I. Primer

6   II. Whirligig

8   III. Wild Horses

12   IV. Mr. S's Magic Dice

14   V. A Gray Day in Venice

18   VI. Action-painting

21   VII. La Sarabande de l'Infini

26   VIII. Hommage à Satie, le Divo de l'Empire

35   **SENTIMENTAL WALTZ**

41   **CHABRIERIANA**

DÉDICACE

52   I.

54   II.

written for ZOFO

Primer

for one piano, four hands

I.
Primer

WILLIAM BOLCOM
(2014)

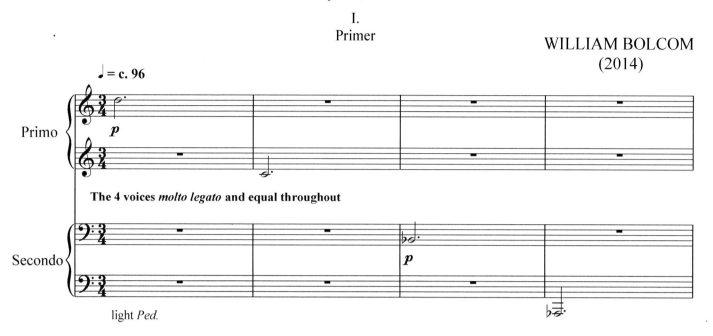

Primo

Secondo

The 4 voices *molto legato* and equal throughout

light *Ped.*

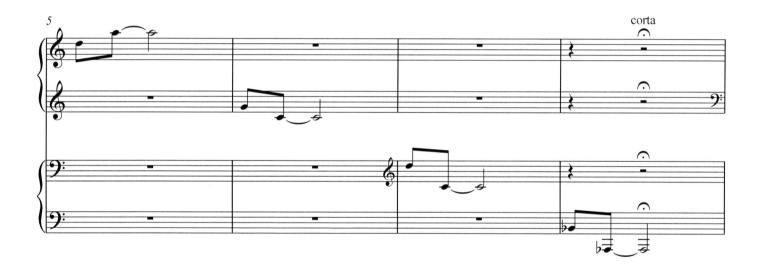

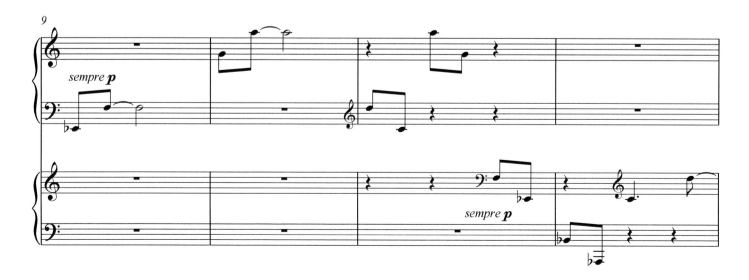

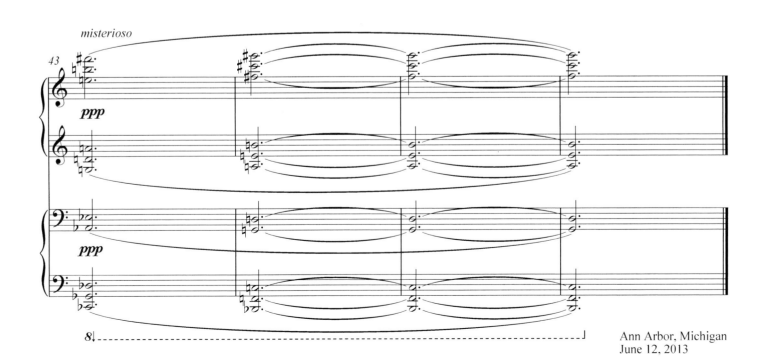

Ann Arbor, Michigan
June 12, 2013

II.
Whirligig

Bloodless and mechanical, ♩ = 68

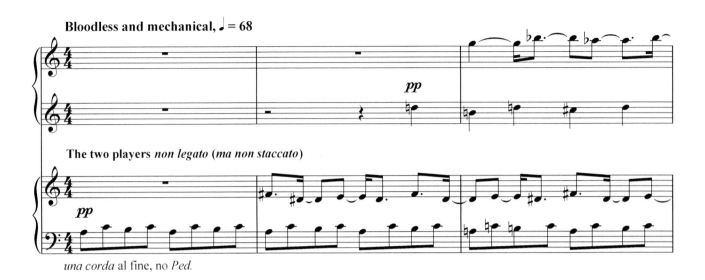

The two players *non legato* (*ma non staccato*)

una corda al fine, no *Ped.*

Linz, Austria - Ann Arbor, Michigan
August 9, 2013

III.
Wild Horses

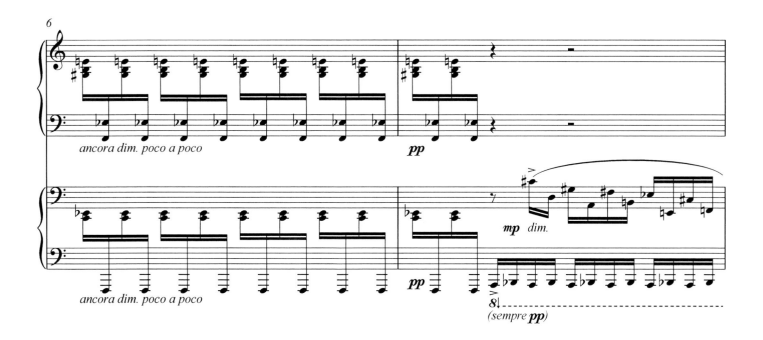

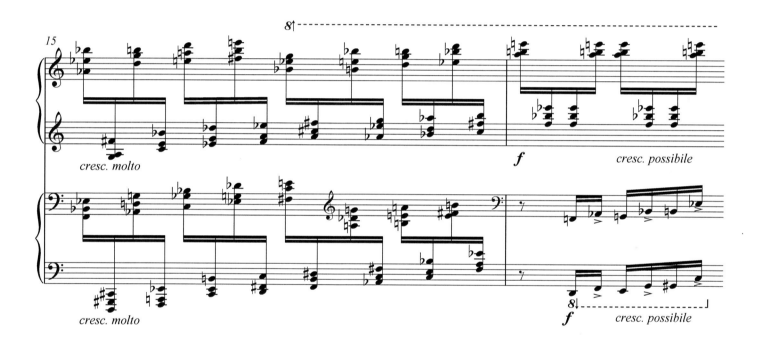

Ann Arbor, Michigan
August 23, 2013

IV.
Mr. S's Magic Dice

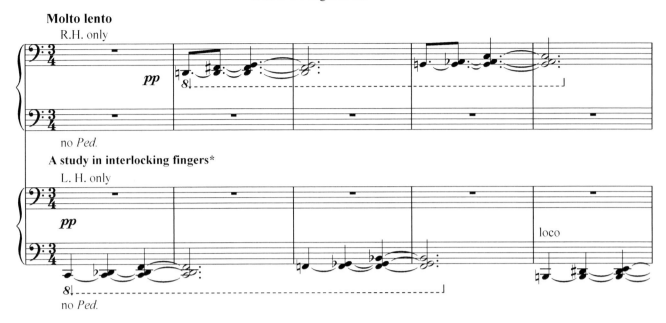

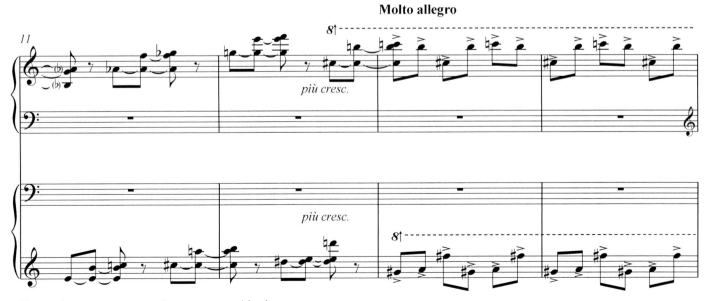

*It may be necessary to stand up to execute this piece.

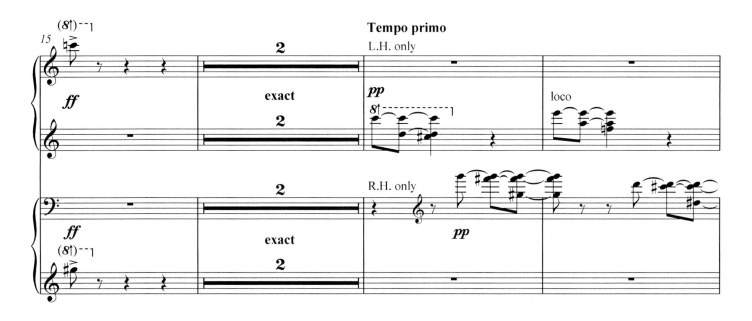

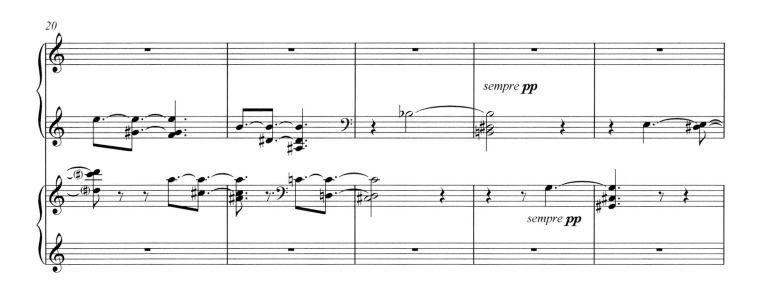

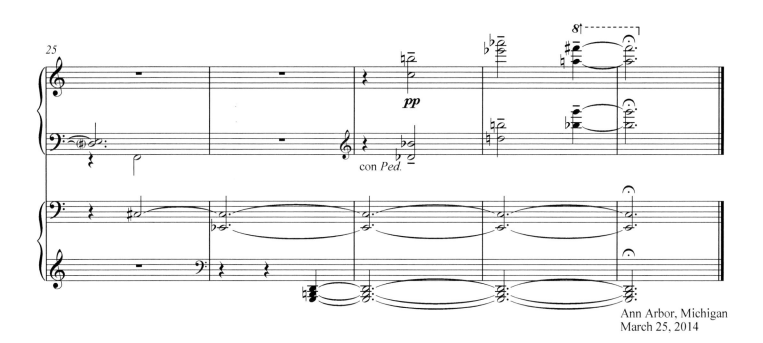

Ann Arbor, Michigan
March 25, 2014

V.
A Gray Day in Venice

Barcarolle Tempo, ♩. = 46

* trattenuto: stretch tempo slightly

Ann Arbor, Michigan
April 25, 2014

VI.
Action-painting

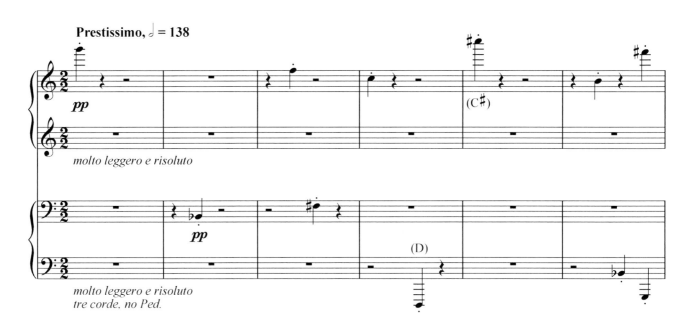

Prestissimo, ♩ = 138

pp

(C♯)

molto leggero e risoluto

pp

(D)

molto leggero e risoluto
tre corde, no Ped.

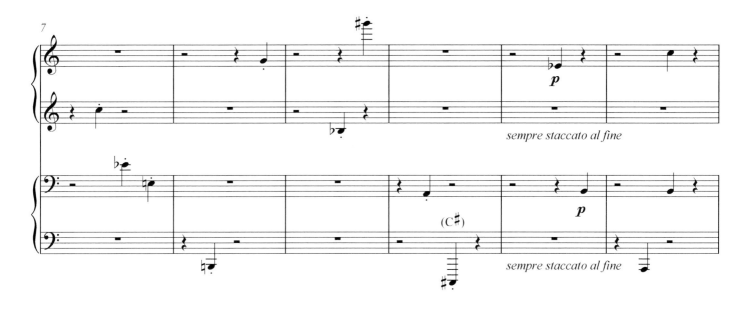

7

p

sempre staccato al fine

(C♯)

p

sempre staccato al fine

13

exact

exact

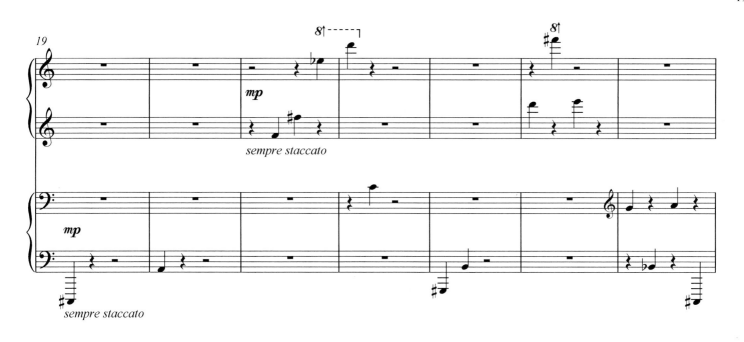

una corda

Ann Arbor, Michigan
May 7, 2014

VII.
La Sarabande de l'Infini

Ann Arbor, Michigan
May 5, 2014

VIII.
Hommage à Satie, le Divo de l'Empire

Finale: Cakewalk montmartrois, ♩ = 74

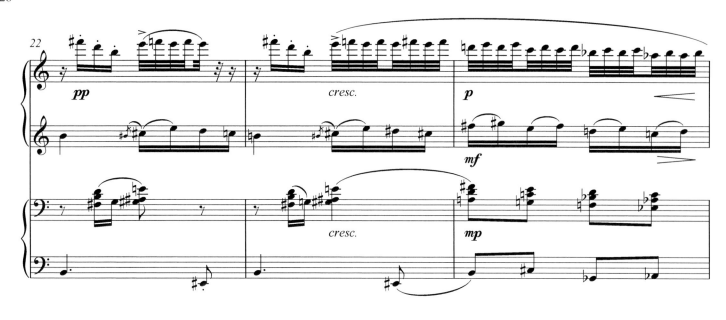

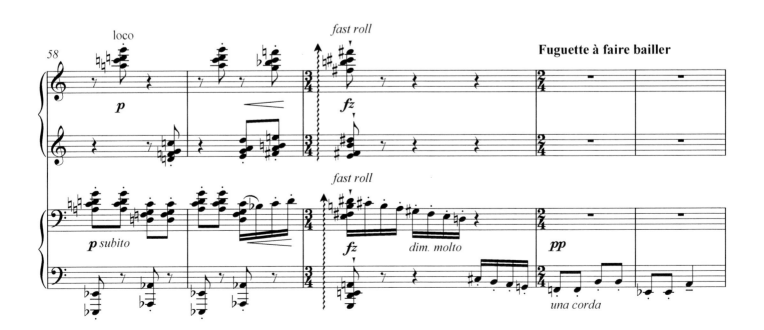

Fuguette à faire bailler

Ann Arbor, Michigan
May 11, 2014

for Luigi Terruso, in memory of Emery Harper

Sentimental Waltz

WILLIAM BOLCOM
(2013)

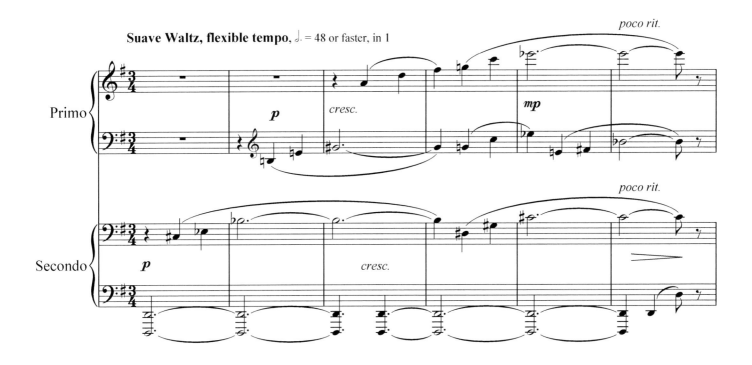

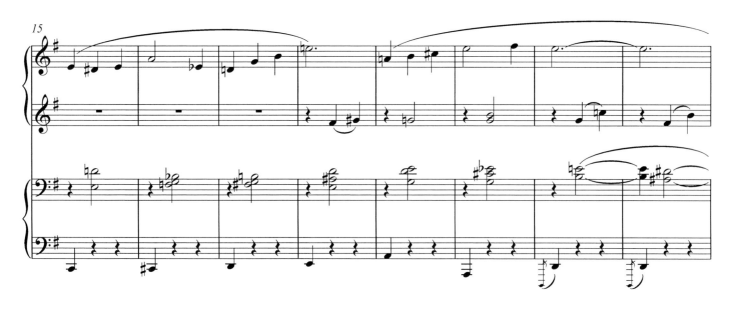

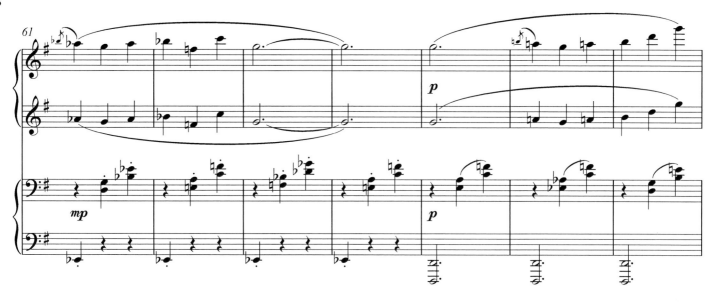

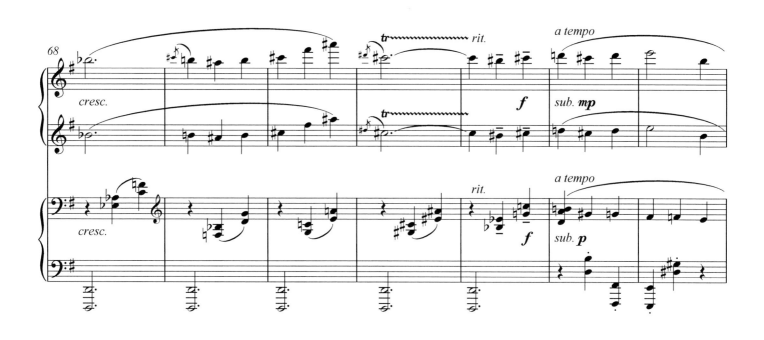

Ann Arbor, Michigan
January 16, 2013

for Guy Livingston, with a tip of the hat to Mark DeVoto

Chabrieriana

WILLIAM BOLCOM
(2013)

NB: This music is written in homage to Emmamnuel Chabrier (1841–1894) and does not contain quotes from his work.

1er couplet

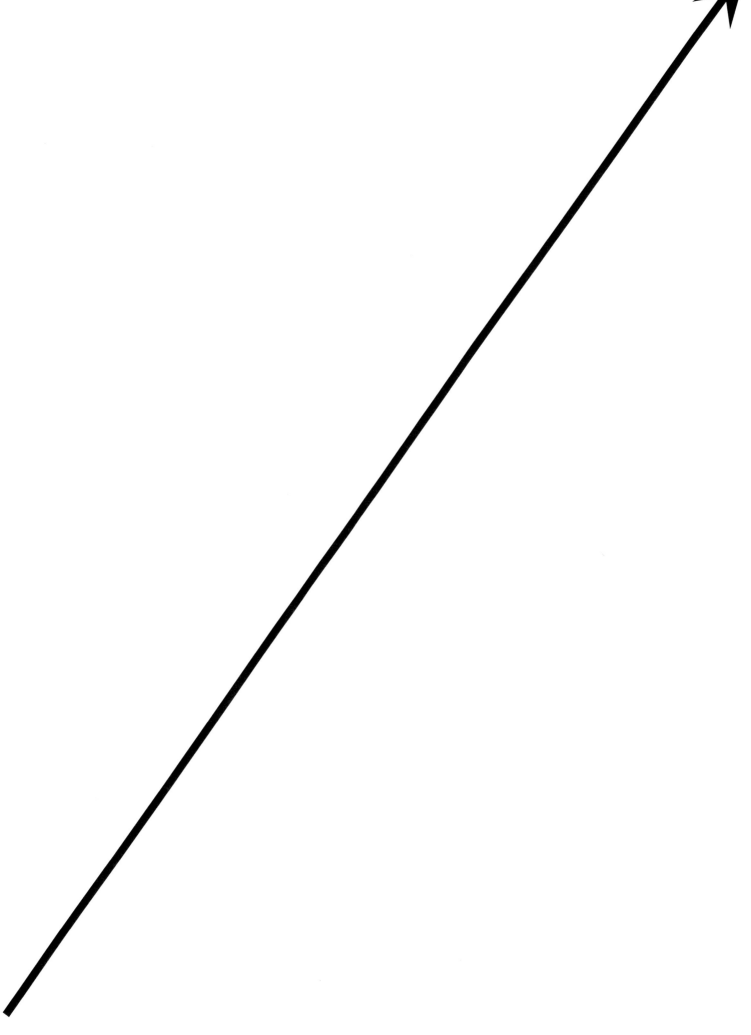

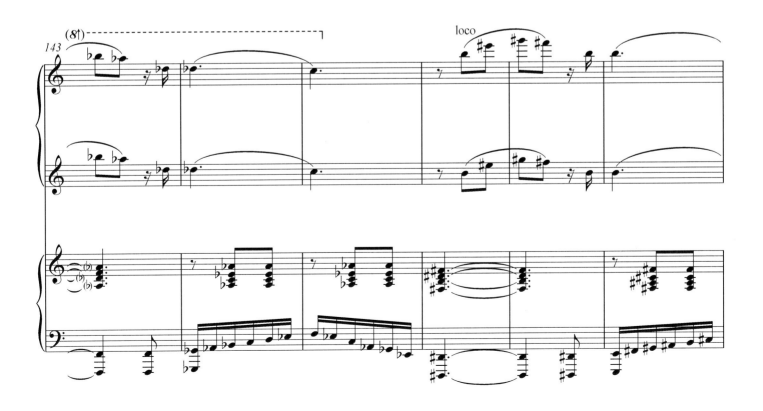

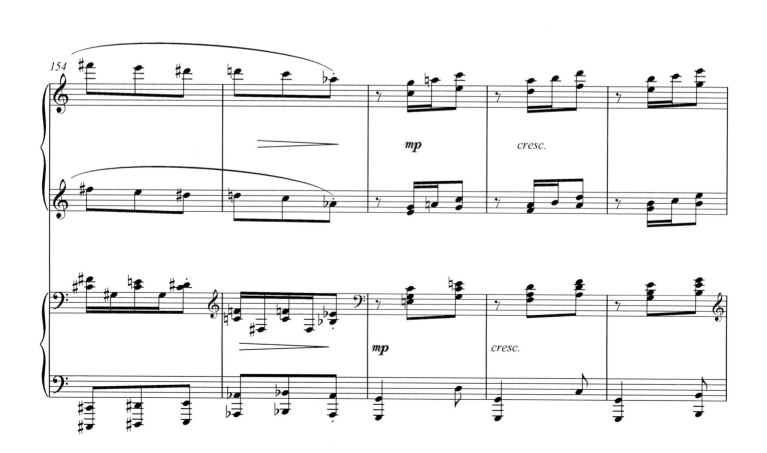

In memory of Darius Milhaud
And for my old friends and co-students of D.M.
- Corky & Barbara -*

Dédicace:
a small measure of affection

I.**

WILLIAM BOLCOM
(1992)

*Content Mont-Smith Sablinksy and Barbara Rowan Wu.

**Each piece can be played as an introduction to another piece; the two pieces can also serve as "bookends" to a group of small works, or for the whole recital.

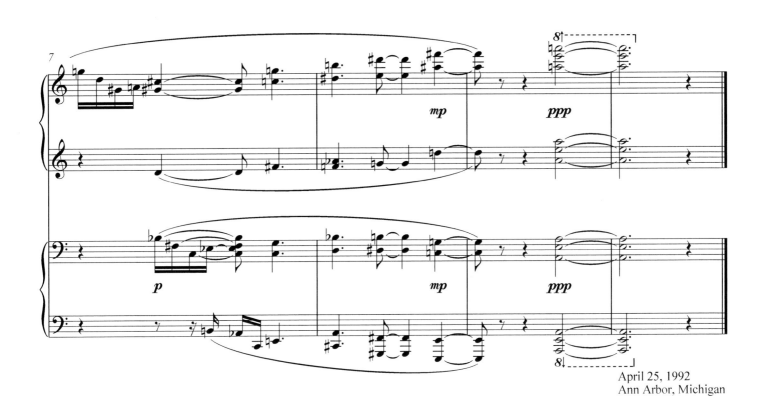

April 25, 1992
Ann Arbor, Michigan

II.

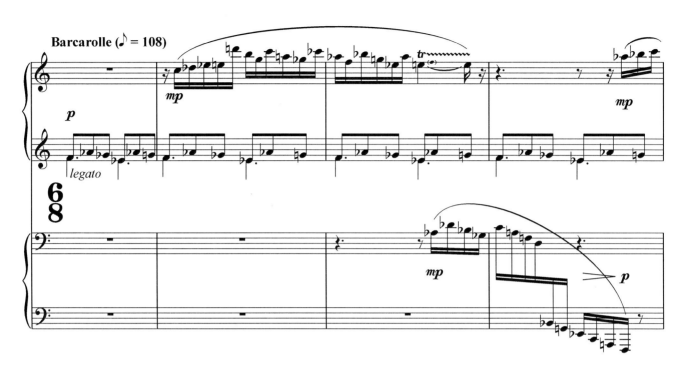

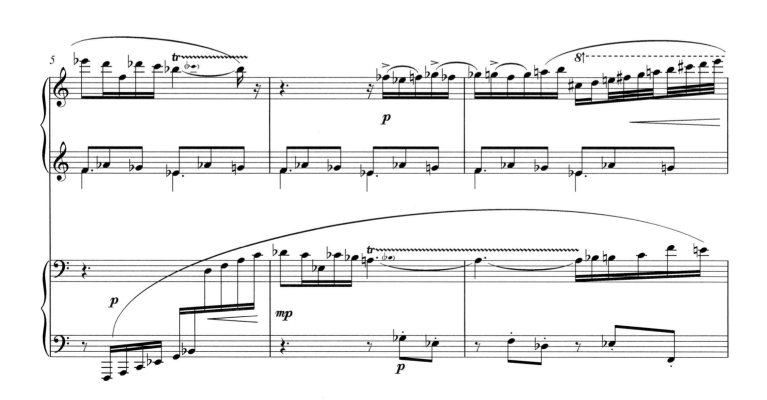

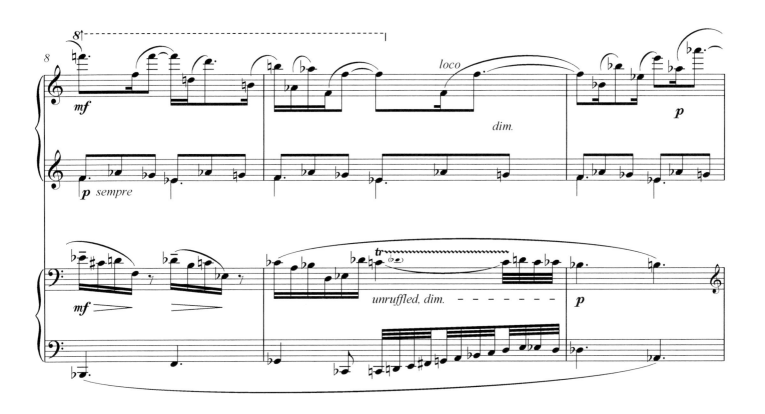

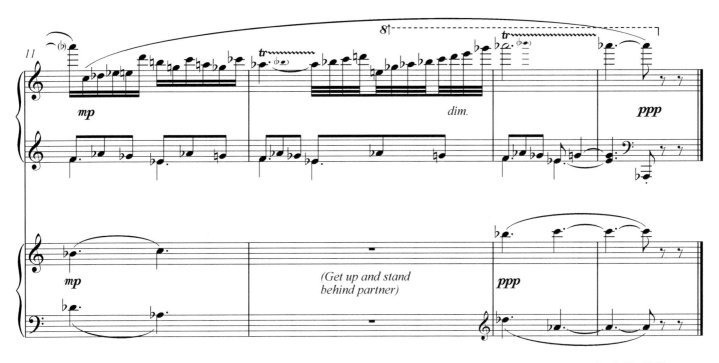

April 25, 1992
Ann Arbor, Michigan